JAZZ SKETCHES

Musical musings on the mother lode

Jon King

Copyright © 2014 Jon King

All rights reserved. No part of this book may be reproduced in any manner whatsoever without the author's written permission.

Printed in the United States of America

For Suzanne. For all of that jazz.

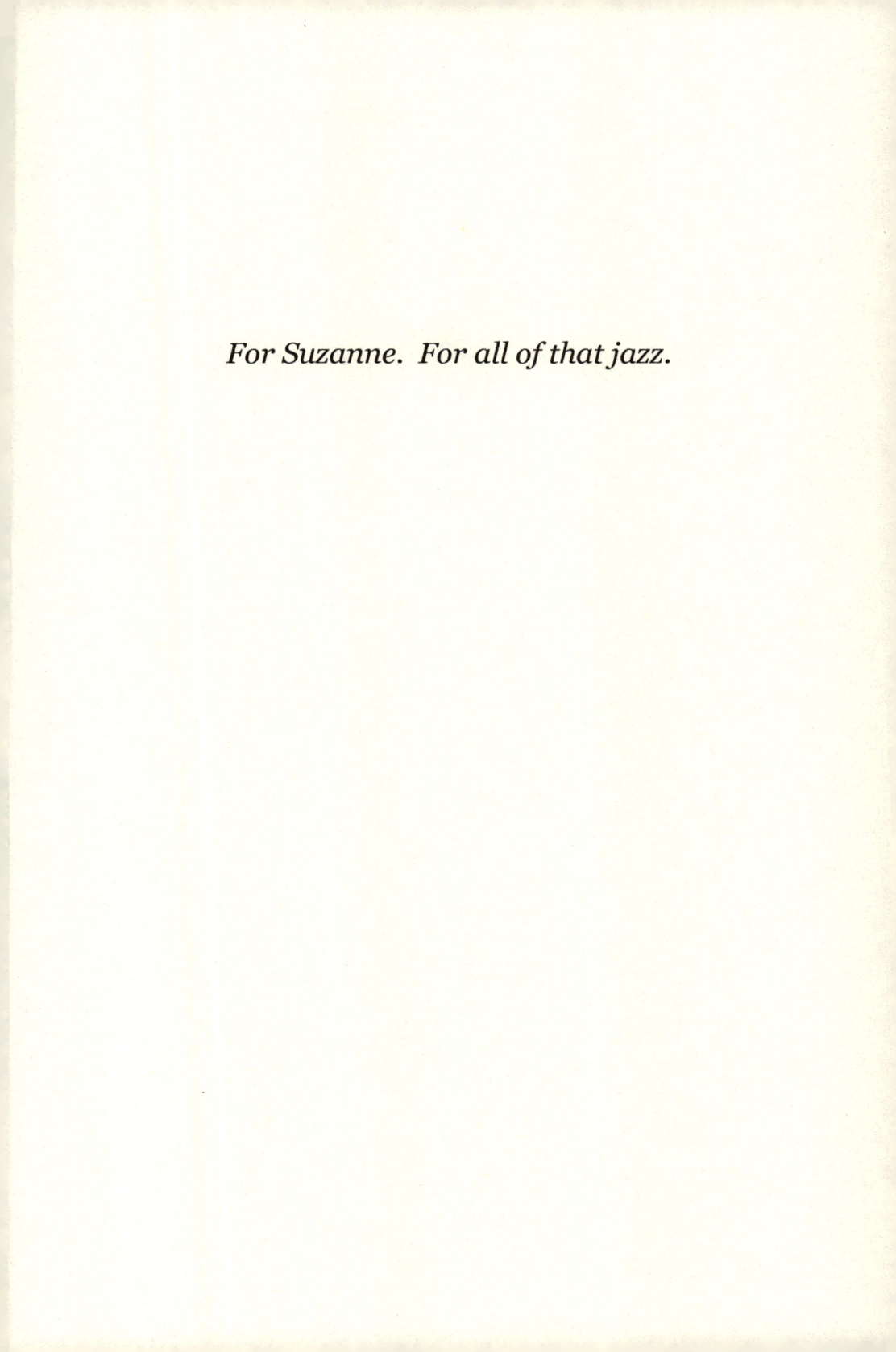

"Kenny, this ain't nothin' but a head arrangement. But let's try it." Something strange happened. The musicians moved stronger, and each played much better than on any of their regular tunes.

From the short story "Head Arrangement," Jon King, 1999

"Introduction" ------

Reading a book on a musical art form is a lot like reading about food. It lacks sensory participation. Which begs the question: Should I have used the audio book format?

No, I'm just too Old Europe to play with any new technology.

So, if you're willing to share some of the good old times that make up this compendium of personal experience, let us go forth.

I promise not to shuck and jive you any more than you are probably expecting. My standard is an old concept: Less is more.

Now, here are other principles I use to organize the book:

- * Adults as "tall children"
- * Not everything of value has a monetary price
- * Music as the highest art

Let us give praise to those famous and anonymous who have unknowingly contributed to this hot mess that I call "Jazz Sketches."

A friend used to default to his own value standard: "Judge someone by what he hasn't done, as much as by what he has."

On the whole, Dear Reader, maybe we each can think of this as an early holiday present.

Hope you enjoy.

"Jazz" ------

One important point is a working definition of jazz. There are long scholarly expositions defining jazz. I prefer a shorter and straight forward definition found in Henry Martin's *Enjoying Jazz*.

"Jazz is a twentieth-century music originated by black Americans and characterized by improvisation and a strong projection of rhythm."

If you are ever in an argument or even a friendly exchange over a piece of music's "jazzness," just apply the template of improvisation and a strong projection of rhythm. I think you will not go wrong in most cases.

"Nature and Nurture" ------

Ever hear of the term "Escape Velocity?" This was an idea advanced by Charles Portis in his novel, *The Dog of the South*. The main character was beset with a feeling that he could never reach his potential during his mundane existence, because he could not attain escape velocity. I read this novel almost twenty years ago. It was supposed to be a work of great importance. Let's consider this theme of escape velocity as it relates to us.

Dream of being like your heroes? Or heroines? Suppose those heroes or heroines were quite different by virtue of race, education, geography and overall culture from you. Some of my earliest heroes and heroines were mystically apart from me. My abilities were those of a typical middle-class, white kid in the Midwest. My interests were a bit more ambitious than making good grades or being a sports star. I played trombone in the fourth grade. I liked Dixieland music. My first jazz record came from the local Safeway store for a couple of bucks. Small price to get hooked, but I was. So, the seed was planted early. Musical snobbery was an early weakness. I began to realize a lifelong struggle to join the ranks of those first heroes, to somehow achieve escape velocity in the fourth grade.

One of the first setbacks I suffered was during the fourth grade band concert. I was walking up the steps to the stage at school and tripped and fell smack dab in the middle of my trombone slide. It was no longer my first concert. It was my first brush with failure. I have blanked out what I did during the program that night. I think that I just sat there on stage and didn't play a note.

(It should be noted: In some forgiving way I continued to be in the band, and I wielded a new replacement slide made possible by my practical, middle-class parents.)

"Clark" ------

CT was my first modern jazz-playing hero. No Dixieland, just stone chops and fly technique. I was now in senior high school. I wanted to play like Clark. So did a lot of guys. He was in a category by himself.

Why was Clark such a major trumpeter? Why was he so special?

His playing was unmistakable.

Clark's environment was witheringly poor growing up. He made his first trumpet out of a junked garden hose, and he spent his youth in unenviable conditions. I had to put down his autobiography after these details. It was depressing.

To look at Clark, you would guess that he never had a care in the world. He was a stout, hip-talking cat who had happiness etched on his face. And more than that, he sounded happy. He could play choruses of magical notes without pausing to take breaths. He perfected a technique called circular breathing, by which he kept playing while taking in air to keep playing – or something. Never could do it myself.

Clark told of apprenticing on the riverboats on the Mississippi River as a very young musician. He told of having to play for incredible lengths of time, show after show. I still have the image of the peg legged tap dancer he mentioned in his memoir. I think that he grew up as he shifted for himself.

He also described being a victim of racial bigotry in the Old South. He responded to this professionally, by becoming the first black musician to be a regular in The Tonight Show band during Carson's heyday.

"Mumbles" was his signature vocal piece. Clark scatted, using nonsense words of his creation, to keep the show moving with his happy-go-lucky flair.

He enjoyed working in a number of the best bands of his era, including Basie and Ellington. Also, Clark impressed many of us with his work with valve trombonist Bob Brookmeyer in their poll-winning quintet during the '60s.

I'm sure he made a difference to me along the way. Clark Terry – master.

"Roots" ------

Some existentialist writer whom I stumbled upon during college (see PJ O'Rourke's reference to his school: a non- or not-so-competitive Midwestern state university – *The Baby Boom*, 2014) made an impression. He felt that everyone needed an "ultimate concern." His theory related to how we would experience more of life's joy, if we had such a thing. This concept makes sense to me. How else could I justify writing this personal stuff? Do not our passions and interests form our standards, our ethics, our essence? I believe they do.

Growing up in the Midwest, as did O'Rourke, we shared a few concerns like Vietnam and aging comfortably. I think PJ's concentration upon writing must have been his response to wanting to leave home for far-flung places to cover (see escape velocity). My essential choices revolved around music, but with similar long-range goals.

"Did you hear the one about the rabbi who saved all of his clippings?"

Poor taste you probably say. Allow me to attribute that zinger to one of my teenage influences, my music teacher Jay. He taught me how to play trombone from splat to tasteful, even though his jokes were sometimes R-rated. Jay was cool.

Jay helped me to get a new horn from the music store where I took private lessons from him. That horn, according to the story I was told, was specifically built to be used by the big band leader Si Zentner (see "Up A Lazy River"). So you see, I was on the fast track, at least in my opinion.

I played that horn all through high school, one year in college, and quite by accident and luck, in an Army band after college.

Jay was cool, as I said. He drove a Karmann Ghia convertible, smiled a lot, loved jazz and didn't care what anybody else had to say on those subjects. I think "cool" was his ultimate concern. I even got to play a couple of dances with his group as a high school kid.

Perhaps what I really treasured from Jay's lessons were his occasional interjections of advice on things non-musical. One example was how he responded to my news that my practice schedule had been interrupted. I had to mow my weekly lawns that my dad thought were necessary in the summers. Jay looked at me seriously and said, "I don't know. Don't you have your whole life ahead to make money?" Cool.

I also had a special high school band teacher. He taught me to play better each year by running a solid program that included a stage band class three times a week. That band was great preparation for the work I did with the 1st Infantry Division Band about four years later.

"Jack" ------

The phone rang after I had finished my homework. It was a school night, and I had gone to bed. The call was for me. One of my junior high classmates self-consciously, as though being prompted, said, "Do you want to go hear the mighty T? My dad wanted me to ask." This turned out to be my first and only encounter with "the father of jazz trombone." He was leading a group of top-notch players and working a dance at the local country club. This was a culture shock for me. I got the okay from my parents and got dressed. A huge salmon-colored convertible with white leather seats picked me up for the set. That family included me that night, because their son and I were in a school Dixieland band together. We arrived about 10 p.m., and as we entered I was met with a heady combination of tobacco smoke and alcoholic aromas that I had never experienced. The crowd was laughing and talking freely. I had never seen adults acting like these people. After a couple of all-out ensemble statements, the unmistakably rich and nimble playing of the trombonist swept me up, as if I had been hypnotized. At the end of the set, my friend's father, a very sophisticated jazz fan, guided me to the bandstand and introduced me to a jazz icon – a man who had played with the Louis Armstrong All Stars; the man who redefined the limits of jazz trombone; a guy they say played trombone as if it were a trumpet. I met Jack Teagarden.

"KC" ------

Recently, I had a short e-mail contact with a rising star jazz pianist whose work impressed me on one of his CDs. In response to my unsolicited compliments, he wrote, "I can't wait to get back to Kansas City and get my hands on some Kansas City barbeque." Gracious fellow. My point is that some cities have it going on for jazz.

Kansas City holds some interesting memories.

"Ooh, Lou," the woman's voice ecstatically echoed across the rows in the dimly lit Municipal Auditorium. This was in response to Lou Rawls' announcement that he was about to sing the Lennon McCartney tune "Yesterday." Also, at that same event, a loud male voice rang out in mocking urban style, "You better hang it up, sookie, sookie!" in response to a lesser known female singer, lacking the stature and natural abilities of Mr. Rawls. What a thrill it was to witness my first Kansas City Jazz Festival in the mid-'60s. Also, what a thrill it was to be in attendance with a friend who drove us the sixty miles in order to get there. (I had not yet received full driving privileges from my parents.)

Unfortunately, the tradition of The Kansas City Jazz Festival has been replaced by other events which may have greater mass appeal. This decision is lamentable and needs to be recalibrated for those of us who miss the fun at 13th and Central, downtown. In fairness to younger Kansas City leaders, they deserve credit for staging the annual 18th & Vine Jazz and Blues Festival and several other jazz "festivals" throughout the year.

There is one more concern at this point. Do you know that the word "barbeque" not only means a certain cultural cooking method, but also can be an urban reference to a desirable young woman? (as in the song title "Struttin' with Some Barbeque" – Louis Armstrong, et al)

"Bill" ------

William Jefferson Clinton, kudos for being the first "jazz president."

President Barack Obama, kudos for being the second one.

"Brotherhood" ------

Not all of my musical exploits were exciting.

I spent a lot of time sitting in rehearsal rooms, sight reading concert band parts, counting symphony part rests while the strings played, and marching. Oh, marching! I always disliked it. I never felt that it liked me either. It always seemed like a track and field event – not music. Marching really got to be a hassle as my smoking increased and my drinking followed the same curve.

However, Dixieland was another subject. I played in two different school-organized bands. During junior high, we were in a parade downtown, riding on a flatbed truck (not marching).

Another time, my high school group was asked to provide an atmospheric element at a state candidate's political rally in the nearby university town. The event was held in a stately old hotel in the downtown loop. We all wore our homemade, but uniform, red and white striped blazers and either costume-type derbies or skimmers. Anyway, I remember we were well received. During the one break we took, we were milling around the lobby, and a black man came up to us and acknowledged our performance. We had an extroverted clarinet player who did our talking. He said, "Hey, this gentleman wants us to stop by his room upstairs." So there we were in this fellow's chamber and he asked, "Would you all like a drink?" (while pouring Scotch into his own glass) I think we all passed on the offer, but he had another request. "You guys are really good. How would you like to tour Japan with my group?" Not only did I not drink, but also I still had homework that weekend for high school. The clarinetist wanted more details however. It turned out this hip-talking guy was one of The Drifters and was performing at the popular bar across the street from the hotel.

I stayed in school, but felt a kinship with this performer. Brotherhood of man and such.

"02E20"* ------

Have I mentioned Vietnam? The 1st Division? Here's my story, and I'm staying with it. All the lessons, the practicing, the school marching bands sort of helped me into a lucky spot at a challenging time in my life. I had been drafted. I had turned down the offers for OCS (Officer Candidate School) and had decided to cast my fate to the wind – militarily.

It so happened that I was doing KP in the mess hall, which was very normal for all troops to do when their turn came up. I was in the sights of a very power-hungry cook who was borderline crazy. This guy had me going until he finally grabbed my t-shirt at my neck and clenched his fist as if ready to punch. I calmly asserted my sense of survival and reminded him that he would be in the brig for such a reckless act. Then, not too much later, another soldier with sergeant stripes approached me and asked, "Would you like to come with me and try out for the band?" No brainer! Anyway, I was lucky, and I played marches and concert pieces that I had played before in school.

The whole band tryout had been originated, because I had completed one of the blank spaces on a form that asked if I had any special skills, the first day at the induction center, eight weeks earlier. Hell, yes! I played the trombone.

I had mixed emotions writing this episode. On one hand, I realized that I needed to be careful not to treat the military inappropriately. On the other hand, some of the experiences weren't so good. They were great!

I was stationed at a fort not far from home (60 miles). I had to serve two years. Most of the bandsmen had enlisted and had signed up for three years. I had not prepared to teach music like many of my fellow troops. The unit also included a stage band. What's more – I got to play in it.

Accordingly, I've included one of my happier military duties.

The band was ordered to accompany the other units of the division to a regular training exercise in Germany. Okay, fair enough. We all were anticipating a glorious musical sweep through Deutschland. It turned out that this was foolish of us. Instead, we found ourselves doing guard duty and KP in the forest there. No instruments, no playing, just soldier stuff. Until one evening a USO tour came to our camp to entertain us. The featured act in the show was a young Asian woman who was closely chaperoned by a showbiz-looking, young Caucasian, leading man type. The woman was a singer, but she didn't have a live group to back her up. Ta-daa, we were the combo! The singer launched into the Gershwin tune, "Summertime," and we did our best to find the key and follow her lead. I remember I alternated between two notes played meekly, but with attitude, as the bass line, while the trumpeter did the melody. What a multicultural effort: an Asian singer, doing a Jewish composer's song, accompanied by a group of Midwestern bandsmen in Germany.

As fate would have it, I got to man the 2nd Trombone chair in our unit's stage band. I even took a couple of short choruses in two tunes during our Fourth of July outdoor concert in 1970. Big fun.

*02E20, my MOS (Military Occupational Specialty) – Trombone Player

"Aesthetics & Subjectivity" ------

Perhaps you agree that "one man's trash is another man's treasure." I would like to consider this concept as it relates to jazz journalism.

I have found that some jazz critics are distinguishable by their approaches, from highly academic to boringly trite. The same distinctions apply to serious jazz authors. You can be put off by too much technical jargon and not enough precise language, as you try to understand a complicated jazz solo or composition.

To be fair, there are plenty of deserving writers who seem to get it.

One of my favorite books on the topic of jazz is *Enjoying Jazz* by Henry Martin, Macmillan, 1986. Unfortunately, it is out of print. However, you should try Amazon for a list of sources for used or even new copies.

Another example of substantive jazz writing is the book, *The 101 Best Jazz Albums: A History of Jazz on Records* by Len Lyons,

1980. It is out of print as well. Try Barnes & Noble for used copies.

Otherwise, check works by Ben Ratliff, Ira Gitler and Leonard Feather.

One other observation: Be prepared to pick your own favorites.

There is a great degree of subjectivity in being a jazz fan.

Two examples of subjectivity in my own case illustrate my point.

I was newly discharged from the Army and wanted to learn jazz at a school. In those days, I knew my choices were Berklee in Boston, North Texas State in Denton, or Indiana at Bloomington. After some serious decision tree modeling and one unfortunate tryout, I ended up in none of the above.

I had decided on Indiana for financial and other personal reasons. So I headed out and showed up for an audition at the school in Bloomington. I have few vivid memories of that place: a giant, three-dimensional Stroh's Beer billboard at the gateway to the town; a rude waitress at the first restaurant that I stopped at; and a hangover.

I was sitting in my motel room, and the room phone rang. It was a guy whose parents knew mine and had heard from them in our hometown that I was there to try out. "Let's get together for a beer tonight." Okay, we started on the Pabst Blue Ribbon (PBR) by the pitcher at a student bar. I think we ended up closing the place after a few more PBR pitchers. Next morning, I felt like my head was about to crack, and my mouth was like a dry well. (Never miss the water until the well runs dry.) The tryout took place early in the morning. I found out a month later that PBR and jazz school were mutually exclusive. Someone (namely the school faculty) had gotten subjective with me.

Gillette, Wyoming is definitely not known for its jazz. I lived there and worked for the local newspaper as an advertising sales rep. I had my family in tow, so I had become more vanilla, as they say. Anyway, there was an occasion that surfaced that involved jazz.

A local FM rock station had a weekly Sunday night jazz show hosted by a community lady.

This woman had heard that I liked jazz and called me to bring in some of my own records to play on the show. It was amusing to play some jazz that came from my collection for the audience that night. I hope it did not cause the listeners too much culture shock. One comment by my host that evening was, "That really didn't flip my skirt, but hey, that last one was something else!" (comparing a Gillespie track to an extended live cut from *Nina at Newport*) That was considerably subjective.

To continue using the idea of subjective judgment, I have listed some of my favorites and why they are.

* Gerry Mulligan Quartets –
  Classic Mulligan cool jazz with Chet Baker or Bob Brookmeyer.
* Blood, Sweat & Tears –
  Changed the landscape by pioneering jazz-rock.
* The 3 Sounds –
  Old school, Gene Harris-led, soul jazz trio.
* The Charles Lloyd Quartet ('67) –
  Set a new standard for small group jazz improvisation.

* The Jazz Crusaders –
  Fresh hard bop sound, excellent soloists.

"Live vs Studio (Recordings)" ------

Any fan who listens to a wide sampling of recorded jazz has to make some listening decisions. Studio or live is perhaps most basic.

Studio recordings that were originally made before 1960 were apt to have rather inadequate percussion fidelity. So, nowadays, it's wonderful to get a remastered CD of those early sessions. I have this opinion, because of my fondness for the drums (percussion) in jazz. I think a person can almost accurately guess when a specific track was first recorded by analyzing the drummer's style and the recording's fidelity. Pre-1960, it seems the drum was a neglected instrument in the engineering of many albums.

Now, let's tackle the desirability of live recorded vs. studio recorded.
I choose "live," because it involves more unfiltered content than studio work. It's fun to hear an occasional audience hoot or chuckle, and more interesting, occasionally, to gauge your opinion in comparison to an

audience's applause. "Live" tracks are often more extended and encompass more room for soloing and exploration of the song.

In other words, to answer the question sometimes asked by band leaders during extended soloing: "Shall we give the drummer some?" (a drum solo) Yes, of course.

Another reason that I love "live" is that in many cases the combinations of musicians are more interesting than those on studio dates. For example, live at Newport recordings are often one-of-a-kind, concerning players involved. The same goes for many live at Montreux performances.

One caution: Try to avoid poorly engineered live recordings and studio dates. Listen for a good balance in the sound mix.

"Gene" ------

Pianos were tested, when they were played by this man. He could play with so much soul that it may never be matched. He played in Kansas City on several occasions that I attended. Always smiling during his long excursions into the melody, or while laying down his signature rhythmic comps, he was a crowd pleaser as well as a great player. I think that in the late '60s I saw my first dashiki, when Gene sported it in an outdoor free concert at a Kansas City park.

Gene Harris. You should check him out on "You Make Me Feel So Young" on his CD, *Like a Lover*, Concord '92. I think you may be amazed.

Amazing indeed! Let me list a few other recordings that I regard as definitive.

* Stan Getz, "I Remember Clifford" from *Dynasty* CD, Verve, 1989
* Buddy Rich, "Billie's Bounce" from Very *Live at Buddy's Place* CD, Groove Merchant, 2009

* Jimmy Witherspoon, Gerry Mulligan, Ben Webster, Jimmy Rowles, Leroy Vinnegar, Mel Lewis, "Goin' to Kansas City" and "See See Rider" from *Live at The Renaissance,* 2012, available from iTunes
* Manny Albam and His Jazz Greats, "Somewhere" from *West Side Story/Steve's Songs* CD, Fresh Sound, 2009
* Nina Simone, "Born Under a Bad Sign" and "Chauffeur" from *The Definitive Rarities Collection – 50 Classics,* 2009, available from several online sources

"Denver" ------

Like many large cities, Denver fosters the arts and cultivates a jazz scene. I spent ten years there sampling its wares.

Mile High City miscellany? Of course, there's more to tell.

Fits and starts is how I remember working in Denver. I was always trying to earn more money to provide the basics for my family's needs. My wife became the essential bread winner, and I smiled and shuffled along selling newspaper advertising in several suburban markets. If soul came from dues paying, I was soulful. During my days selling ad space, I commuted to work on I-25 to Castle Rock about 25 miles each day. It was a beautiful trip. That was because I had the car radio tuned to a wonderful low signal radio station, KADX-FM, broadcasting jazz exclusively. By chance, the station's studio was also in Castle Rock.

One afternoon in Castle Rock, I stopped by the station and met Mr. Dick Gibson. Mr. Gibson was the same gentleman known for his annual Vail Jazz Party that featured famous jazz players from New York, Los Angeles and many other meccas. In fact, the "jazz party" idea was his own invention that became a staple in the scene across America. I hope I have accurately conveyed his incredible wit and his wonderful work with the following examples.

Dick was the morning drive time personality. One morning, he told an extended tale that lasted for what may have been five minutes. It was attributed to one of his musician friends who had told the joke.

(I have paraphrased the story) Hitler was hunkered down in a bunker, rockets and explosions were going off all around. (more description) One of Hitler's officers entered the bunker and stumbled before the *Führer*. (description) He gasped for breath and reported, "Sir I'm sorry to say that we are losing the battle badly, our troops are being decimated, (description) and it looks very grim for you and our commanders." Hitler cast an acknowledging glance and uttered, "You know, days like this can really give you the blues." (I almost wrecked my car while laughing.)

Gibson had great concerts that he staged in downtown Denver at the Paramount Theater. He loved to present famous players and combine them in unusual ways just for these shows. The music was more than most of the audience expected. Gibson used to quip that these bands were so good that "I could get them work in Jersey." He was devoted to jazz, and we all were his beneficiaries.

One other Gibson story involved Sarah Vaughan. He was promoting her as one of the featured concert artists at the Paramount. He paused and concluded the announcement by revealing how Ms. Vaughan had a passion for red shoes. That was why he always bought her a new pair of red shoes, whenever she worked for him.

I miss Gibson. He left us in 1998.

"Souvenirs" ------

Commodified experience. Commercial exploitation, some is good, but only in moderation. That is my opinion.

First, let's define the term "Commodification" as "the transformation of goods and services, as well as ideas or other entities that normally may not be considered goods, into a commodity."(Wikipedia)

My first awareness of the danger of commodification came a few years back. A book I had read lamented the filtered, watering down of the Chicago blues club scene through a guided bus tour for fans that explained in scripted language to its passengers what the music and performers were all about. This replaced going inside the club to listen. Why? Anxiety about racial conflict, fear of drugs or cultural influences, or conservative prejudices may have contributed. Possibly, commodification may be due to a gradual loss of individual spirit from unused instincts for adventure and first-hand experience. (Think cable television. If we don't climb a mountain, we'll watch it being done by others.) Anyway, let's be careful not to exchange life's joys for the sake of being more secure or out of fear of external circumstances like a blues club in an urban setting like Chicago.

I can remember taking a cab to a well-known jazz club in Washington DC about fifteen years ago. I was eager to show my wife the real side of live jazz that night. Our driver asked where we were wanting to go. I explained. He hesitated and said, "I don't know if you want to do that. Some cabs won't even go to that part of town." I persisted, and he agreed to our plan. Upon arriving at the club, we were struck by unique graffiti adorning the picket fence along the street. The driver advised us to be careful and leave before the club closed. We were so engrossed in the music that we ended up leaving after the last set. At least I was engrossed. My wife was visibly frightened by the whole experience and unfortunately returned to our hotel and regurgitated before bed. I was sorry for this, but I value that evening to this day.

I confess I love kitschy stuff. My collected jazz and music-related items include: an album cover signed by my hero, the late Bob Brookmeyer, obtained while at a Kansas City jazz club performance; a George Wein-signed Newport Jazz Festival program from 2013 (Mr. Wein established the festival in 1954 and is still its muse currently); a Newport Jazz Festival cap, a Newport Jazz Festival 2013 poster; a pair of folding lawn chairs featuring the New Orleans Jazz & Heritage Festival logo 2010; numerous concert programs scattered in drawers and on shelves in my house; and t-shirts. The value of these items may be very slight, but they represent a lot of effort on my part, and I never intend to abandon this form of commodification.

"Nina" ------

I dig this singer.

From the first time her music was played on a Kansas City radio program and I fell asleep to "I Loves You Porgy," to catching her in concert during her final US tour in 2000, she moved me.

Her career was wide-ranging and took her to Europe, Barbados and venues like Newport, Town Hall and Carnegie Hall in the states. Anticipating a new release on RCA, Phillips, Colpix and other labels was like a natural high. Her material was often relevant to the civil rights movement, and it was commonly criticized for being too radical. I found her to be a source of idealism and strength in that confusing era.

I collected her albums, new and used. At one point I had over thirty on my shelf. I read her autobiography. I argued her style and distinctive vocal approach with anyone who questioned her worth. I discovered more inspiration for writing and music from her than from any other source. From my perspective, Nina was the gold standard of jazz singers. To further canonize her here is unnecessary.

Nina Simone, the consummate artist, lives.

"Honorable Mentions" ------

These lists will help to show what specific recordings, concerts, and jazz clubs rank as favorites.

Jazz recordings since 2000:

* Karrin Allyson, *Ballads: Remembering John Coltrane*, 2001
* Mike Longo, *Explosion*, 2002
* David McMurray, *Nu Life Stories*, 2003
* Various artists, *Fusion for Miles: A Bitchin' Brew*, 2005
* Bill Frisell, *Big Sur*, 2013
* Natalie Cole, *Natalie Cole en Espanol*, 2013
* Chick Corea, *The Vigil*, 2013
* Jaimeo Brown, *Transcendence*, 2013

Jazz Concerts:

Chick Corea with Gayle Moran. A standout performance by Corea that I remember for his amazing keyboard skills and his unbridled physical stamina. His tempos ranged from pensive to rousing, and his duets with Moran were well conceived and highly creative. I will always consider this a lifetime experience.

The Dizzy Gillespie small group. This concert is memorable for unusual circumstances. Dizzy's sidemen that afternoon were young talents that he had assembled to fan his creative impulses. These guys were as dissimilar racially as they were in age from Dizzy. I don't remember all of them, but I think there was an Asian and at least one Caucasian. The weather outside was icy and snowing heavily. This caused the show to be delayed for over thirty minutes. The delay was because Dizzy's trip from the airport was affected by the icy roads. As the emcee tracked the group's arrival, he assured the audience that we would soon be joined by the band. In strode Diz, dressed in a heavy wool overcoat, a stocking cap, and a wool scarf that wrapped around his neck and trailed behind him. He walked all the way across the stage and stepped to the microphone. Smiling his usual way, he started to improvise his story. He said that the weather was the worst that he had ever experienced. "You have to have (several examples of courageous individuals) and the fortitude of Paul Robeson to make this trip (from Kansas City)." For whatever reason, the music, while very good, seemed incidental to Dizzy's words.

The Paul Winter Sextet. This was one of the best small bands I experienced as a youngster. The band performed in a high-ceilinged chapel with exaggerated acoustics. Bossa Nova was their core message. They had just returned from Brazil and had been strongly influenced with that burgeoning style of music. Wonderful ensemble work and terrific soloing highlighted the show, especially a 10-minute drum workout wherein the other band members paid their respects by leaving the stage until it ended. That solo was by Ben Riley, and it is the best that I have ever experienced.

Louis Armstrong & The All Stars. Of course! Early in my developing musical life, this group was a true epiphany. The band featured brilliant improvisation, fine dynamics, and virtuosic musicianship. I knew my level of playing at the time was crude in comparison. This band represented the finished product in every way.

Blood, Sweat & Tears. I was completely spellbound by their group intonation. (all perfectly in tune with each other) It was such a joy to hear eight or nine players "speaking" as one instrument almost like a pipe organ. Their fusion of jazz with rock rhythms whetted my appetite for more.

An Evening with Natalie Cole. Just over a year ago, my wife and I attended this musical masterpiece. It was an evening kickoff to the Newport Jazz Festival 2013 and was staged at the International Tennis Hall of Fame in a very large outdoor setting. There was seating for the crowd of over 3,500. From our seats located about twenty rows up in a "classic" wooden grandstand, the music mixed with the cool night breeze almost intoxicatingly.

This show was a triumph! The music grew better, song after song. Great arrangements and excellent programming rocked the house. I think "Oye Como Va" may stick in my mind forever. (The wooden grandstand experience will never be matched either.)

Jazz Clubs:

I tried to list at least five favorites and failed. I have been to a small number of jazz clubs over the years, so the sample size was limited. My first selection was Ralph Gaines' place in the Union Station in Kansas City. I stalled because that was now irrelevant, out of existence. Then I listed another club and stopped for the same reason. This fact points to a sobering conclusion: Jazz clubs are fragile things. They start and stop more frequently than many businesses. They change their entertainment format to other types of music such as rock or country and western. Their founders and owners die. I suppose this fragility comes from the business organization. No corporate financing. Small business status. Lack of commercial entrenchment. Whatever it is, jazz clubs come and go.

Here are my two favorites that I know still exist:

El Chapultepec in Denver

Dimitriou's Jazz Alley in Seattle

"The Long Haul" ------

Music appreciation can be healing. The blues was originated by slaves to alleviate the burdens of slavery. Try the blues to counteract your own "mind-forg'd manacles." It's also wise to remember the blues is a fundamental root in jazz music.

Therefore, spare yourself. Listen to the blues to help cure the blues.

About twenty years ago, I was a fairly sick fellow. I went to the emergency unit at a Denver hospital, explained my problems, and eventually went home with a new lease on life – heart bypass surgery. I'm very grateful for that hospital and its excellent doctors.

To be truthful, this episode was painful, both physically and mentally. One source of relief that I received immediately in that recovery unit was listening to my portable CD player and a Nina Simone CD that my wife had the profound wisdom to bring to my bedside. That was some very good medicine.

"Fandom" ------

> *1: all the fans (as of a sport) 2: the state or attitude of being a fan – Merriam Webster online*

Are you a fan? What's your team? Yankees? Disney? Who are your heroes and heroines? Mantle? Minnie Mouse? We're all members of the big fandom. Whether it is music, or sports, or entertainment, there are fans.

Over the course of my jazz encounters I've had the distinct pleasure of being in the company of many interesting and beautiful people. These folks are typically fun to be around and tend to be happy with their existences. Not shy about showing their approval, they are often quite effusive. These jazz fans are everywhere. Jazz fans appreciate literature and the fine arts. Most of them are aware of the good in humanity, in all of its expressions.

From my perspective, it's easy to be a fan. It's a lot of fun.

"Where are you heading musically?" I asked the drummer sitting at the counter at a

Denny's. I had applauded him earlier that evening during a Blood Sweat & Tears concert and was very impressed. He turned to me and responded, without much animation, "I think we're going to Des Moines."

See you around.

JK

For your feedback:
OneForAllFund@gmail.com

Appendix ------

This article was published originally in *JAM, Jazz Ambassador Magazine*, the magazine of the Kansas City Jazz Ambassadors.

It appeared in the June/July 2000 issue.

Old Wine, New Millennium
Picking Jazz Recordings To Go
By Jon King

(Ed.Note: From time to time we receive requests from people who are discovering the joys of jazz and are in need of a list of recommended recordings. While there are many different ways to skin that cat, here is one JAM reader's take on some essential albums both novice and pro alike can enjoy.)

"Why don't you write a piece listing your indispensable jazz recordings?" my wife prompted me, as she observed my struggle with self-discovery.

And so I did.

I am a jazz fan. But not a jazz critic. That would be hypocritical, given my belief that reading about jazz is like reading about food.

To me, so-and-so's rehash of xyz's rendition of "Body and Soul,' in which the music is described as "devilishly virtuosic," makes no hay...even if the writer is, um, virtuosic. My reading about jazz kindles only two responses: 1.) I wish I could play, and 2.) jazz is a business, after all. So, that's why I prefer my innocence. And my fan status.

Picking my favorite offerings turned out to be no trifle. And I apologize if my methodology seems biased. Remember, I'm simply a guy who happens to love jazz. Also, my choices appear to underrate certain styles: Dixieland, swing, and free jazz in particular. Fans can be like that. Maybe I can explain it better by saying that my favorite recordings sport an ingredient of magical surprise – original, pure, connect-with-the-listener surprise.

I highly recommend these works. You will hear magic.

- Louis Armstrong – *Ambassador Satch* (1956), Columbia CL 840

- Shelly Manne & His Friends – *My Fair Lady* (1956), Contemporary S-7527

- Stan Getz/J. J. Johnson – *Getz & J.J. at The Opera House*
  (1957), Verve 831 272-2 ('86)

- Gerry Mulligan – *Paris Concert*
  (1957), World Pacific WP-1210

- Bob Brookmeyer – *Kansas City Revisited*
  (1958), United Artists UAS-5008('84)

- Louis Armstrong – *Louie & the Dukes of Dixieland*
  (1960), Audio Fidelity AFSD 5924

- Art Farmer/Benny Golson – *Meet the Jazztet*
  (1960), MCA/Chess CHD-91550('90)

- John Lewis – *The Golden Striker*
  (1960), Atlantic SD-1334

- Gerry Mulligan – *Gerry Mulligan and the Concert Jazz Band on Tour w/guest soloist: Zoot Sims*
  (1960), Verve V/V6-8438

- Andre Previn – *West Side Story*
  (1960), Contemporary S 7572

- Nina Simone – *Nina at Newport*
  (1960), Colpix CP 412

- The Three Sounds – *Moods*
  (1960), Blue Note 4044

- Pee Wee Russell/Coleman Hawkins – *Jazz Reunion*
  (1961), Candid 8020

- George Shearing Quintet w/Nancy Wilson – *The Swingin's Mutual*
  (1961), Capitol Jazz CDP 7 99190 2 ('92)

- Horace Silver – *Doin' the Thing*
  (1961), Blue Note 4076

- Mel Tormé – *Comin' Home, Baby*
  (1962), Atlantic 8069

- James Moody – *Great Day*
  (1963), Argo LP-725

- Paul Winter – *New Jazz on Campus*
  (1963), Columbia CS 8864

- J.J. Johnson – *Proof Positive*
  (1964), Impulse A-68

- Oliver Nelson – *More Blues and the Abstract Truth*
  (1964), Impulse A-75

- Shirley Scott – *Queen of the Organ*
  (1964), Impulse GRD-123 ('93)

- John Coltrane – *The John Coltrane Quartet Plays*
  (1965), Impulse A-85

- Eddie Harris – *The In Sound*
  (1965), Atlantic SD 1448

- Jimmy Smith – *Organ Grinder Swing*
  (1965), Verve V/V6-8628

- Clark Terry/Bob Brookmeyer – *Tonight*
  (1965), Mainstream S/6043

- Gary McFarland – *Profiles*
  (1966), Impulse A-9112

- Sonny Rollins – *Alfie*
  (1966), Impulse A-9111

- Charles Lloyd – *Love-In*
  (1967), Atlantic SD 1481

- Kenny Clarke/Francy Boland – *Fire, Heat, Soul & Guts*
  (1968), Prestige PR 7634

- Buddy Rich – *Mercy, Mercy*
  (1968), World Pacific ST-20133

- George Benson – *The Other Side of Abbey Road*
  (1969), A&M SP 3028

- Thad Jones/Mel Lewis – *Central Park North*
  (1969), Solid State SS 18058

- Quincy Jones – *Gula Matari*
  (1970), A&M SP 3030

- Larry Coryell – *Larry Coryell at the Village Gate*
  (1971), Vanguard VSD-6573

- Stan Getz – *Dynasty*
  (1971), Verve 839117-2 ('89)

- Buddy Rich – *Very Live at Buddy's Place*
  (1971), Groove Merchant GM 3301

- Gene Ammons – *Gene Ammons and Friends at Montreux*
  (1973), Prestige P-10078

- Conte Candoli/Frank Rosolino – *Conversation*
  (1973), RCA TPL1-1509

- Cedar Walton – *A Night at Boomer's, Vol. 2*
  (1973), Muse MR 5022

- Stan Kenton – *Kenton '76*
  (1976), Creative World ST 1076

- Phineas Newborn, Jr. – *Back Home*
  (1976), Contemporary OJCCD-971-2 (C-7648) ('98)

- Cal Tjader – *At Grace Cathedral*
  (1977), Fantasy F-9521

- John Klemmer – *Nexus*
  (1979), Arista/Novus AN2 3500

- Weather Report – *8:30*
  (1979), Columbia PC2 36030

- Miles Davis – *We Want Miles*
  (1982), Columbia C2 38005

- Freddie Hubbard/Oscar Peterson – *Face to Face*
  (1982), Pablo 2310-876

- Maynard Ferguson – *Live From San Francisco*
  (1983), PAJ PA 8077

- Shelly Manne – *In Zurich*
  (1984), Contemporary C-14018

- Archie Shepp/Chet Baker – *In Memory Of*
  (1988), Optimism, Inc. LR CD-5006

- Mose Allison – *My Backyard*
  (1990), Blue Note CDP 7 938402

- Barry Harris – *Live at Maybeck Recital Hall, Vol. 12*
  (1991), Concord Jazz CCD-4476

- Gene Harris – *Like a Lover*
  (1992), Concord Jazz CCD-4526

- Gerry Mulligan – *Rebirth of the Cool*
  (1992), GRP Records GRD-9679

- Lou Rawls – *Portrait of the Blues*
  (1992), Manhattan CDP 0777 7 99548 2 7

- Karrin Allyson – *Sweet Home Cookin'*
  (1994), Concord Jazz CCD-4593

- Great Guitars (Byrd/Kessel/Ellis) – *Great Guitars at Charlie's Georgetown*
  (1994), Concord Jazz CCD-4209

- Dave Brubeck – *Dave Brubeck Jazz Collection* (1995), Legacy/Columbia C2K 64160

- Lonnie Smith – *Purple Haze* (1995), Musicmasters 01612-65135-2

- McCoy Tyner – *Infinity* (1995), Impulse IMPD-171

- Kevin Mahogany – *Kevin Mahogany* (1996), Warner Brothers 9 46226-2

- Dizzy Gillespie – *Bird Songs, The Final Recordings* (1997), Telarc CD-83421

- Eddie Harris – *The Last Concert* (1997), ACT 9249-2

- Andy LaVerne Quartet – *Four Miles* (1997), Worldly Triloka 314 536 186-2

- Michel Petrucciani – *Both Worlds* (1997), Dreyfus Jazz FDM 36590-2

- Keith Jarrett/Gary Peacock/Jack DeJohnette – *Tokyo '96* (1998), ECM 1666 78118-21666-2

- Oscar Peterson/Benny Green – *Oscar & Benny* (1998), Telarc CD-83406

- Etta James – *Heart of a Woman* (1998), Private Music 01005-82180-2

- Chuck Mangione – *The Feeling's Back* (1999), Chesky JD 184

Reprinted with permission

Made in the USA
Coppell, TX
17 April 2022